AN ARCHITECTURE

Chad Sweeney

BlazeVOX [books]

Buffalo, New York

An Architecture by Chad Sweeney

Copyright © 2007

Published by BlazeVOX [books]

All rights reserved. No part of this book may be reproduced without the publisher's written permission, except for brief quotations in reviews.

Printed in the United States of America

Book design by Geoffrey Gatza

First Edition

ISBN: 1-934289-68-X   ISBN 13: 978-1-934289-68-6
Library of Congress Control Number: 2007938738

Cover photograph by David Holler

BlazeVOX [books]
14 Tremaine Ave
Kenmore, NY 14217

Editor@blazevox.org

publisher of weird little books

BlazeVOX [books]

blazevox.org

2   4   6   8   0   9   7   5   3   1

ACKNOWLEDGMENTS

Grateful acknowledgments to the editors of the following journals in which sections of *An Architecture* have appeared, sometimes under different names or numbers:

Backward City Review

Coconut, editor Bruce Covey

Colorado Review

Interim

Mirage #4 Period[ical]

New American Writing

Parthenon West Review

Ping Pong

Shampoo

Slope

Several sections were featured in a film exhibit by artist/film maker Eric Zener at the Hespe Gallery in San Francisco, March 2005, and one section appeared in the chapbook *A Mirror to Shatter the Hammer* (Tarpaulin Sky Press, 2006) as the poem "Landscape."

Special thanks to friends and mentors who were excellent readers of this manuscript: Paul Hoover, Maxine Chernoff, David Holler, Jennifer K. Sweeney and James Maughn.

for Jennifer Kochanek Sweeney

AN ARCHITECTURE

It rests in change.

By the speed of its change, it scatters

and gathers again.

—Heraklitus

1

every year
the statue grows heavier

I want to put it down
on this clover hill overlooking

the library
it might roll away from me

it wouldn't be my fault
if it broke back to its four colors

its mound of shells and water

2

bridgework

wedgework

signwork

seedwork

3

the library is burning
fire reads aloud

in Arabic in Greek

translating each book
into smoke

outside we climb the sidewalks
past windows that fill

with our presence
up
stairways   thru doors

the invisible limps beside us

millions of *is* and *is not*
posture and stride   in

faith a man
holds tight

to his own leash

as rain

falls
and does not fall

4

Though railroad tracks appear to meet
in the distance

they never do.
Hired mourners depart

to the wrong century.
Radio signals

bead along strands of smoke
over Appalachia

(where I feel tempted to report
the rivers are smoldering)

and glaciers in New York Harbor
redirect the lights

straight up into the haze.
Music reinforces the girders.

One must

rely on hypnosis,
a window

the color of wine
is what in death

terrifies.
The future protagonist

under development,
equidistant from his flaws,

imposes this plot on memory.

5

We searched the cities
              in ones—each

for the other, orphans without

memory, the divorced, the
prisoners—we

ate among cars and wires,
in the concrete was

no mother, in halls ten
floors up no

father—and sent each day
our children

into huge buildings

into rows.   It's
how we lived.

6

taxis heaped with shoes
bees and pages

torn from books—language!
turns

with shipyard birds
in sleeves of

warehouse glass
our city

in green air and high green

light
rush hour under the ocean

each face crowded with
former selves

of the not chosen

7

too vast to render
in watercolors   —the field

recedes

within us
toward a sepia line:

seven archetypes of
catastrophe

the lead swallow   in the flock
changes

now *that* one the others
                    follow

a single billowing

8

I should have said
I meant to say

the flock turns
in that carpenter leaning on the pole

differently than
in you who read it—

at the museum
we file by in ones   pulling

each thing up by its naked
material—plucking it out

into light   from the zero—
the sun

shines for those who demand it, one

scarab, one flint—edge
of the rail, the rail edge

speaks
of an approaching train

its circumstance
and something of the words

shouted in dining cars

9

for a time one may walk
beside herself, but

there intervenes

a street light or
manhole around which she

regathers her step and jostled
by the crowd turns toward

and away from—it's always
both—inserts her body

into the bank turnstile
to deposit her pay

repeating the sentence
her grandmother intoned this

time of year

favoring
the ankle that hurts less, that is

less swollen

10

the nouns are verbs
conduit between *I* and *I*

from which the fish the fowl—
looking

into it
a face

breaks on the well water
source and structure

—the double

helix
a thrush's voice

of the body and be
yond the body

is the meaning of our talk

11

To carve a bird from
a bird,
to make a stone
from a stone.   To have

worked it all day without
obstructing its flight—the flying

stone goes
dark at night and glows not
with light, but its rough
dumb matter

brilliant among roots.

12

by this slow burn
we live

smoldering

a tree

fire inside its wood
walks

out from the forest

                    the burning bush
is a man

in average moments

13

the snake
swallowing

peristalsis of
the world

by which these rooms
are constituted

camouflage

over a city
block   windswept

of copper
leaves   machines and

their math—
the snake
unrolling

its throat cave
(lingual)

births
the wet days

14

the hillside
collapses toward the water
                                          clutches of briar
nettle

inhabit the marsh reeds
cow parsnip

clamors from spring mud

in throaty wombs
bouquets of nails and beaks

green
through last year's

struggle, skeletal of russet
stalks   no memory

of mother—some
colorful windborne ache of seedpod splitting

15

too many choices
give me a shovel and a pit

let it be a stranger pays me

I will bury mountains
in this red sleep

16

the windmill is turning

and its turnings
are turning

17

he carried the baby's body
everywhere in that violin case

until they wouldn't let him enter the school

then he buried the bundle
under a rose bush

at his birth house in Watanga

18

if he
wants it—and

he wants it—
he may not

feed

his child
of his body's milk

19

twins born the morning
they cut off his hands

lean from the bridge to taunt

the monk   clawing
the mud bank for worms

his toes grip the fish hook

~~Dong Hoi~~

20

On the river a village,
no road but that river

to reach it,
among the women one man

selling what he'd sewn in Hmong
pattern

led us back to his hut—*a
woman*

a mother-man, he said,

*my wife died leaving
the children.*   While men

planted rice
the mother-man of Laos stayed home

to weave.   Scars

beetled his forearms—
shrapnel here, he said

gesturing an airplane—*Amerikha*
floated over

when he was a boy
size of this one giggling in his lap

Booooooom!
his face was watching the bombs again

but bore
no anger   smiling out

from the eyes of seven children.

21

Today I saw two old friends
in the street—passing

but did not know them, did
not stop

to talk. No longer the

self
who loved those men

among the crowds, this sidewalk

longer than I thought.
A new clutter to

defend
in new spaces.

22

every man his own orphan

left himself
on the subway platform

counting
his image

one   one
in passing windows

23

if it is winter and not raining
if it is not winter and is raining
if a blue scarf and a warehouse

if it is noon in the waiting
if build it the bridge or she measure
if night in the shape of a tire

if the bridge before we drive it
if the river minutely shifted
if drill bit or rivet the shaking

if sound is the arc of the trial
if the fractal forgets to complete us
if a blue scarf in winter redeem us

24

Retreating, they collapsed bridges
behind them
and charred the summer rye

Across centuries they marched

along waters of their own
nations

—occupied

25

    my solitude
             shaped like a city
    distinct

    from your solitude
             shaped like a city

                a mobile
    hung in bones—

    embalmed in whiskey and the hope
                  of danger—you

    flow across with the crowd

    at the urge of a flashing
    hand—today

    while the cherry the young
    tree wears a storm

    of blossom

    beside the bulldozer and
    wires

26

I sell subscriptions to my daily life.
The violet gleam of girders.
Pain in the shape of industrial pipe

whose center is everywhere
whose smoke is irony.
Worry is proof of my goodness.

I flex my worry and count to seven.
An elegiac music,
tulips yellow the water.

I speak, therefore I are.

27

The meteor shower
inside the man
maintains his equili-
brium.

Chained to a tractor
he dragged away the surface
of the lake
complete with its reflection.

I painted
the stone's
portrait
directly on the window.

It wore a yellow bird.
It wore a fissure, a patch of light.

My brush was a chisel,
where the glass cracked
day leaked in,
elegant and famished.

Please, lie down with me, here.
Consider a hinge made of wind,
the syntax in a field of rye.

28

shuttling between the past

and this wind rearranging
the palms

a purpose

as the hummingbird has
to pull the world

eludes me—

rain
drawing lines on shingles

is art only

if I see it   there
where the window

frames

the clouds the hills
from which a

train appears
the blue lens

of distance   art is

the ghost between us

29

To make stained-glass windows
for the blind

a color whose effect
                    not visual

touch here, the crack

the tooth
of things.

30

Red

is one kind
of caryatid

holding
its roof

.

31

The woman inside the stone
will not be understood

though we may bow
lay fruit on the threshold

and back away.

Steward only
to this body—kinesate—

to flow beneath
                    one's own house

to be seated in that house.

32

crossing the salt   what
fell away   too heavy to carry

the hands first
        then the tongue   losing

in bundles   all memory of wheat

air had no blood
only numbers

              marked the plain
where ants or crows might have been

33

first day of the year
a large silence
locked between buildings

the strangely white
pigeon could not fly I

chased it from the street
to stand lame
between parked cars

34

an architecture:
fire
stands

oxygen
heat
matter

three poles
delicately
leaning

of a child
what she says
and the lines of

force
moving out from her story

35

difficult teaching the Chinese students
plurals, time,
hers apart from *his*
in this language the god is
somewhere else

having set us down in our woman
our man bodies like clay dolls

taught our tongues to draw thin
unbreakable lines between

the tiger and the tiger's mountain

36

when all was spring and the sea
circled itself small

as a swimming pool

the girl grew sleepy
of the whirring shadows of dragonflies

pulled her finger from the hole
the oceans spilled out and covered her

37

words would neuter the land
to ensure the human

as principal actor

pushing a broom and
brush against the clutter

no common language: but

many
wheels

increase!
says the redwinged blackbird

                    increase!   warble the bluets
in the cool of creek shade

38

impossible to recall one forget-me-not
alone—
a blue wool

gathers and winds
the path
under crooked pine—storms

of gravity
split the branches
loose from theory

—the poppies
(I'll not say their color
if you've not

seen them)
flung into spring
from far away

flung like soft arrows
not one of them straight
not one

straight line anywhere—
and that motion
not of circles

but nearly circles   *repeating*
broken under broken from breaking
into rings   or nearly

(were you with me?)
broken of itself toward making
was the sea

39

           To deepen the moment
into which one sees

the metamorphic surfaces
of air and rock—
                coeval.

Thru time the asphodel
foams up

over the cliff
one long root

in the sun.

40

the Palestinian

boy I watched kicking the
ball

deflated

up those
stairs

the narrow winding
                                  of old

Jerusalem is

by now I think
a man

41

[Wailing Wall]

the rock
cut to great square blocks is

rock despite
its use—
        scored
where sword, where fire

the wall is old, of two
millennia—

but the rock
much older
        holds its edge

not the human story
but something else

of the mineral fact

hay tufts and string
twist the swallows' nests   50 ft up
the generations

circle against the sun

all day come the robes
by the hundreds

in the valleys and ridges
of cloth   a platinum luster

bows when the body bows

42

what clothes tomorrow will be worn
how many millions   and who
chosen

alone   and in waves
make history

what words this hour unborn
flock out toward love in elevator light

when the unbroken air
anchors moon in its window

before anyone's left town
before the betrayal

when the fire is folded inside its wood

night when the animals
night when the tunnel

when diamonds lie unfound in the rock

43

The forest is the forest
of language, each tree stands

for something, elsewhere,
lianas and knot holes, innuendoes.

The house

emerges from conversation,
each of us having placed an apple

in the wall, gummy worm,
sugar brick—this is an audience

participation myth. One reader
opens the oven door. The other

shoves her mother in.

44

to be the one to kiss her
to spring the locks and steal

up the steps, quiet as time on marble
flawless as one wing

of a bombed hospital—
to approach that bed at the center of everything

a slaughterhouse, a summer
festival   :   kiss her mouth

not to awaken but to sink her
deeper that her dreams might engender

in minds everywhere young and old

45

                                but the sound
of car wreck
               draws you to the porch
spilling coffee
               barefooted, without sense to compose
your face
               everyone in their grass
dumb and half-made
                       squinting
into dawn
                   chewing
the one shared thought

46

Sunday in Dale Church, Grandpa
alive again

no longer

as minister   but
among us—

worries his brow toward
the altar

      I'm running out
to catch him

the brightness

of ordinary noon
has flattened the houses, set

fire to the slow trees—
What's wrong, Grandpa?

It's

okay, he says—but
behind his eyes

the dream begins to crack

47

Topaz ripens inside its mountain,

a tryst of flies at the window,
the curtain between this world and the next

flutters each time a sparrow
strikes the house.

Memory goes on making,
wax and weft, like a shuttle cock,

the *yes*, the *if*,
a new kind of hero

to swoop down on the safe.
Tell me it was good enough.

Rain whitens a corner
of the stage

where the family is waiting for news.

The past is filling up
and the future is empty.

The mandolin
carved of ice

makes its music by melting.

48

dimensions weave in
cypress light

casting shade the
statements as questions

the lion is white inside the day
breathing sound

of a car alarm
in long wet cords

the fugitive gods

49

and the snake is both—

the impalpable hardness
of water

shifting of its dune toward

our leisure of towels and lotions.
the diamond

fractures into countless
gestures

of picking up and putting down
and the sea rings it   coiled.

no desire

tho it rock and sway
in its nest of coral and distance.

50

gaze of the coal
miner

lithographed

an ovular hole

over collar and boot

subtraction
the instrument sold him

in luminary packages

51

I subtract one color at a time
to arrive at green.

Green cardinal.
Green snow.

This green is excavated
rather than built.

Looking you begin to feel
disappearance

what culture feels when exposed

to time,
a pit

in the air—
a climbing up to

no altar.

The clover,
the teeth of the horses

shine.
Green burns in the green cloud.

52

What falls loose from
history—Helen

only chose

a stableboy
whose full mouth

she bit   whose voice

made her naked stomach
flutter.   She sobbed

inside the ships.

53

Knowledge

of pipes
from the inside   mineral

abides in the vein.
Not enough

to name it   <Cu>   <Fe>
conduct

ivity, melting
                  point, the way

afternoon renders color along
its flecks and pocks
slapping inside the machine—oil
for a necklace:

a new lexicon of nutrients
and poisons

in the roar of that train.

54

Cheyenne surrendered their few

weapons
by request of Colorado

at dawn were butchered
into pelts

and sent to the parade

Above Sand Creek
no tulips bloom in red to claim

the blood

of buried children
unless this wind

is the flower

55

    to the flower
    the bruised snow
                    and ochre

    hinge and hood
    of
          pistil, stamen, bulb

    is not beauty   but labor
                            annealed

    a language of signs

56

Mystery of the grass—one
and many, to make a face of it,
eyes where shadows beat
in natural and random

declivities

the mud decides.
Grass as mirror

    for the growing
doubts in me, or

loves, to make a face

of shifting planes
    the city is—

of what changes and what
      remains—

that quiver
  of instability
 in the molecule
  by which the world
marries itself in the small.

Chad Sweeney edits Parthenon West Review with David Holler and teaches writing in San Francisco, the last seven years with the SF WritersCorps. He is the author of two full-length poetry collections, An Architecture (BlazeVOX), which was a finalist in the Colorado Prize, and Arranging the Blaze (Anhinga), as well as four chapbooks, most recently A Mirror to Shatter the Hammer (Tarpaulin Sky). With Mojdeh Marashi, he has translated the selected poems of the contemporary Iranian poet H.E. Sayeh. Sweeney earned a BA in English from the University of Oklahoma (including a year of study abroad in La Paz, Bolivia) and an MFA in poetry from San Francisco State University. He lives on Potrero Hill with his wife, poet Jennifer K. Sweeney.

Made in the USA